Midlothian
Public Library
14701 S. Kenton Ave.
Midlothian, IL 60445

GRAMMAR ALL★STARS

THE PARTS OF SPEECH

TENNIS COURT CONJUNCTIONS

By Doris Fisher and D. L. Gibbs
Cover illustrated by Scott Angle
Interior illustrated by Drew Rose
Curriculum consultant: Candia Bowles, M.Ed., M.S.

Please visit our web site at **www.garethstevens.com**.
For a free color catalog describing Gareth Stevens Publishing's list of high-quality books, call 1-800-542-2595 (USA) or 1-800-387-3178 (Canada).
Gareth Stevens Publishing's fax: 1-877-542-2596

Library of Congress Cataloging-in-Publication Data

Fisher, Doris.
Grammar all-stars / Doris Fisher and D. L. Gibbs.
p. cm.
ISBN-10: 0-8368-8905-3 ISBN-13: 978-0-8368-8905-5 (lib. bdg.)
ISBN-10: 0-8368-8912-6 ISBN-13: 978-0-8368-8912-3 (pbk.)
1. English language—Grammar—Juvenile literature. 2. English language—Parts of speech—Juvenile literature. 3. Sports—Juvenile literature. I. Gibbs, D.L. II. Title.
PE1112.F538 2008
428.2—dc22 2007033840

This edition first published in 2008 by
Gareth Stevens Publishing
A Weekly Reader® Company
1 Reader's Digest Road
Pleasantville, NY 10570-7000 USA

Senior Managing Editor: Lisa M. Guidone
Senior Editor: Barbara Bakowski
Creative Director: Lisa Donovan
Senior Designer: Keith Plechaty

Printed in the United States of America

1 2 3 4 5 6 7 8 9 10 09 08 07

CONTENTS

Look for the **boldface** words on each page.
Then read the **TOPSPIN TIP** that follows.

JOIN THE ACTION

What Are Conjunctions?

Ken Wong runs out his front door **and** waves to his neighbor Buzz Star.

"Hi, Mr. Star," he calls out **as** he races toward Buzz's red sports car.

"Hi, Ken. Hop in," says Buzz.

"Thanks for taking me with you **so** I can watch my brother Kevin play in the Junior Hot Shots tennis tournament," says Ken.

"I'm happy you could join me," says Buzz, "**but** I'm going to put you to work on TV. Would you like to be my kid reporter today **and** help me announce the match?"

"Are you kidding?" Ken shouts.

"No, sirree," says Buzz. "You know tennis, **and** you know your twin brother. Who could be a better announcer?"

"Being on TV sure sounds like fun, **but** you'll have to tell me what to do," says Ken.

"Don't worry," says Buzz. "I'll help **if** you need me, **but** I'm sure you'll do well."

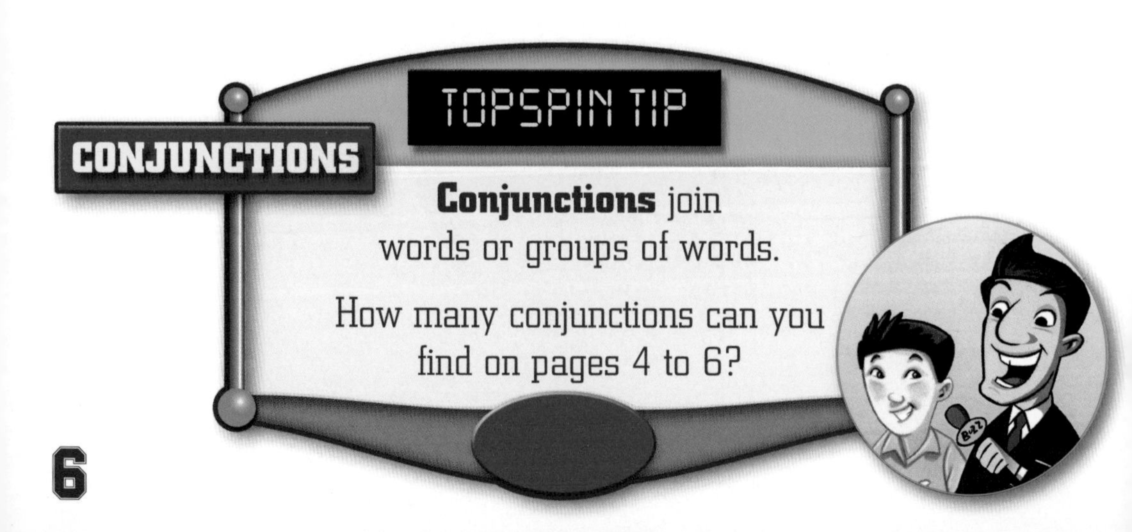

"You **and** Kevin are really good players," says Buzz. "Did your dad **or** mom teach you?"

"Mom **and** Dad don't play tennis," Ken answers. "They signed up Kevin **and** me for tennis camp one summer. My brother **and** I still take lessons."

"That's great, Ken," says Buzz. "Someday, Ken **and** Kevin Wong might be famous tennis twins!"

"Here's the Restless Racquet Tennis Club," says Buzz. "Are you ready to join the action, Ken?"

"I am," says Ken. "I can't wait to watch the match **and** appear on TV!"

"We can sit at court level **or** up in the press box," says Buzz. "You decide."

"I like being up high **and** looking down on the action," says Ken.

"The press box it is," says Buzz.

MEDIA
PASS
BUZZ
MEDIA
PASS

"Kevin is playing a mixed-doubles match, **and** his partner is Bonnie Backspin," says Ken.

"Has Kevin played doubles with Bonnie before?" Buzz asks.

"He usually has a different partner, **but** Bonnie sometimes takes lessons with him," Ken replies.

"Would you like to get a snack before the match, **or** would you rather wait?" says Buzz. "I'm hungry, **and** I see an ice cream stand over there."

"I'm hungry, too, **so** let's order a cone!" Ken says with a grin. "I like chocolate ice cream, **but** sometimes I prefer strawberry. What is your favorite flavor, Mr. Star?"

"I order a vanilla ice cream cone with sprinkles **when** I'm feeling happy," says Buzz. "I like to eat a hot fudge sundae **whenever** I feel sad."

"How are you feeling today?" Ken asks. "Are you happy, **or** are you sad?"

"I'm feeling VERY happy today **because** you are here to help me broadcast the tennis match. It's about to begin, **so** we should get to the press box!"

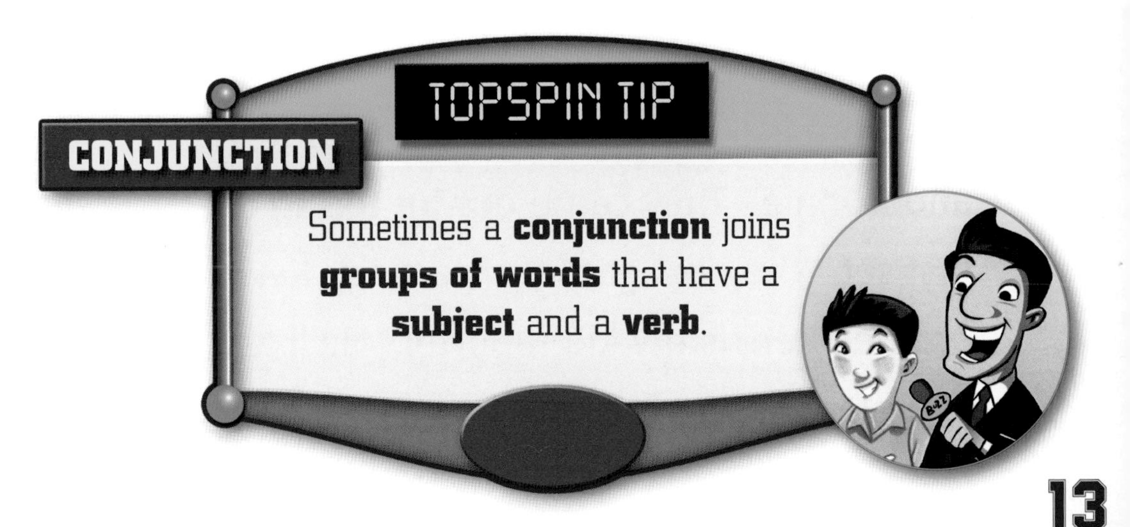

A TIME AND A PLACE FOR A WIN!

What Are Prepositions?

"**For** anyone just joining us," says Buzz, "we're **at** the Restless Racquet Tennis Club. Kevin Wong and Bonnie Backspin are competing **against** Clay Court and Lola Lob **for** the Junior Hot Shots trophy. **In** the second set **of** the mixed-doubles match, the score is 5 games to 4 **in** favor **of** Kevin and Bonnie. They came out **on** top **in** the first set. The next game is starting. Kevin's brother, Ken, is my kid reporter. He'll tell you what happens next."

"OK, Mr. Star," says Ken. "Kevin is serving. He tosses the ball **into** the air and smashes it **over** the net. POW! Clay returns the serve. Bonnie runs **after** the ball and hits it back **to** Clay, but Clay can't reach it! The score is now 15 – love."

Buzz takes over calling the action. "Kevin serves again. He tosses the ball high **above** his head and sends it flying. The ball sails **across** the net and lands **inside** the service box. Lola gets **under** the ball **with** a backhand swing. BOING! The ball sails **over** the net **toward** the sideline.

"Bonnie runs **from** the center **of** the court **to** the sideline. WHAM! BAM! SLAM! The ball is zooming back and forth. What an exciting match!"

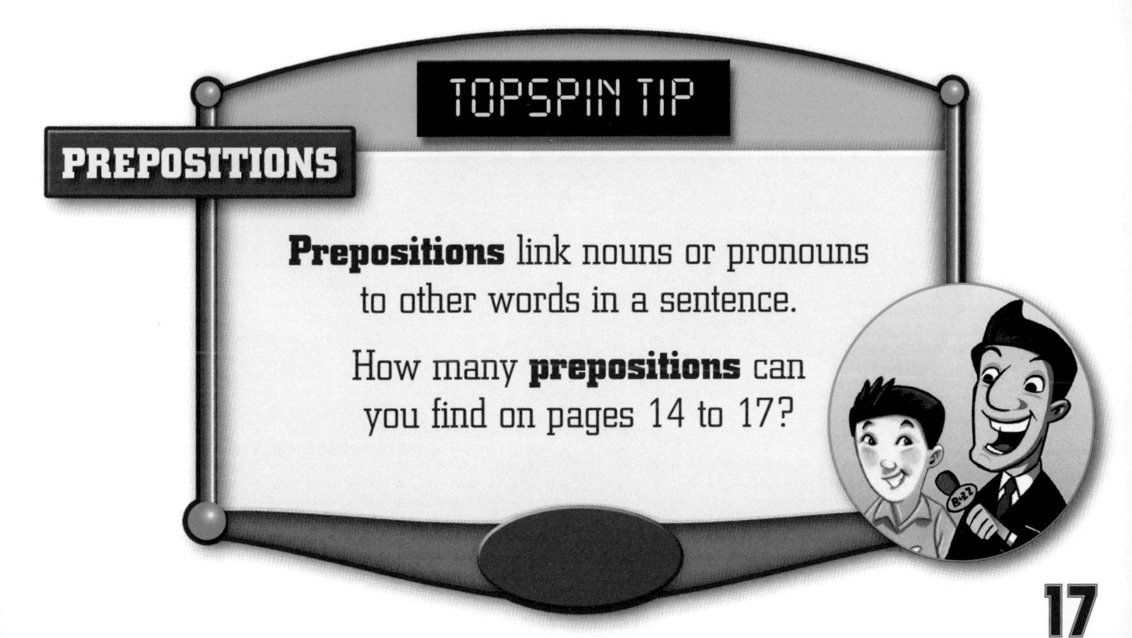

"Uh-oh! Lola just smacked the ball **into** the net, so the score is now 30 – love," Ken says.

"Kevin serves again," Buzz continues, "but Clay doesn't return the serve."

"Your serve was **over** the line," says Clay.

"It was **inside** the line!" says Kevin.

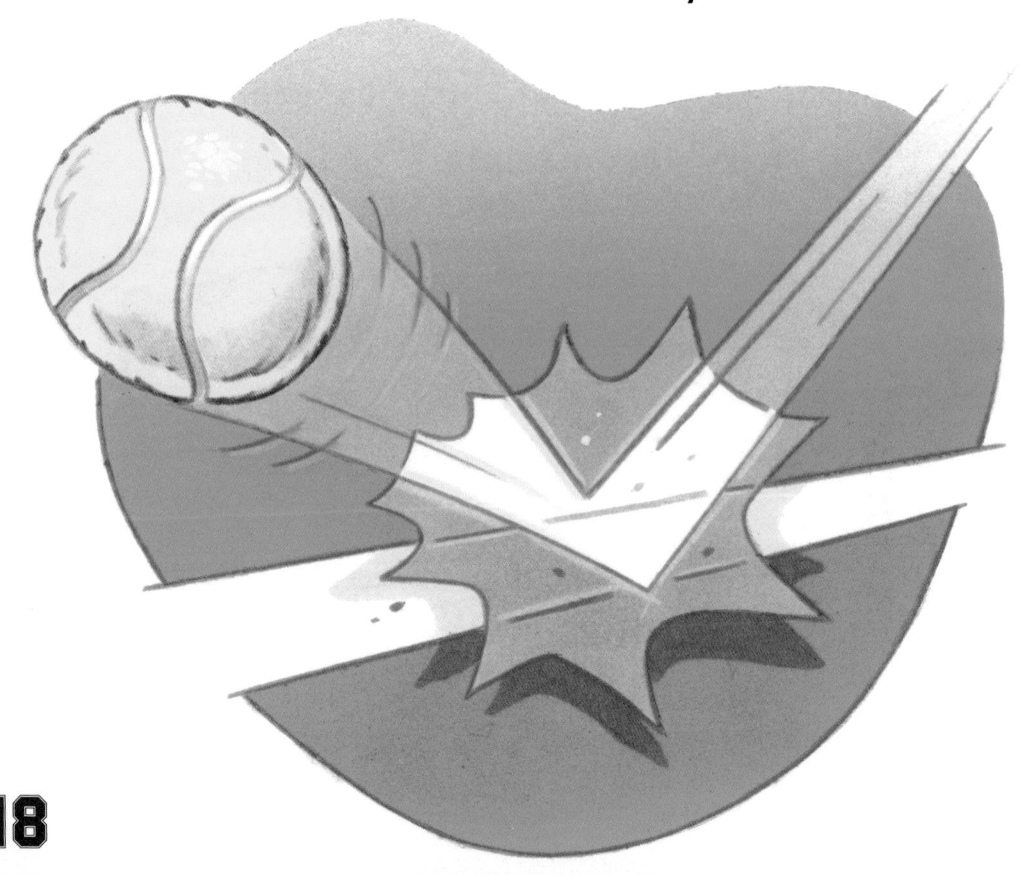

"You're way **over** there," Clay replies. "I could see the ball better **from** here. It flew **across** the line."

"Did not!"

"Did too!"

"Besides," says Clay, "you had a foot fault. You were standing **on** the baseline!"

"Was not!" shouts Kevin.

"Were too!"

"Well, folks," says Buzz, "the line judge says the ball was **on** the line. The score is 40 – love."

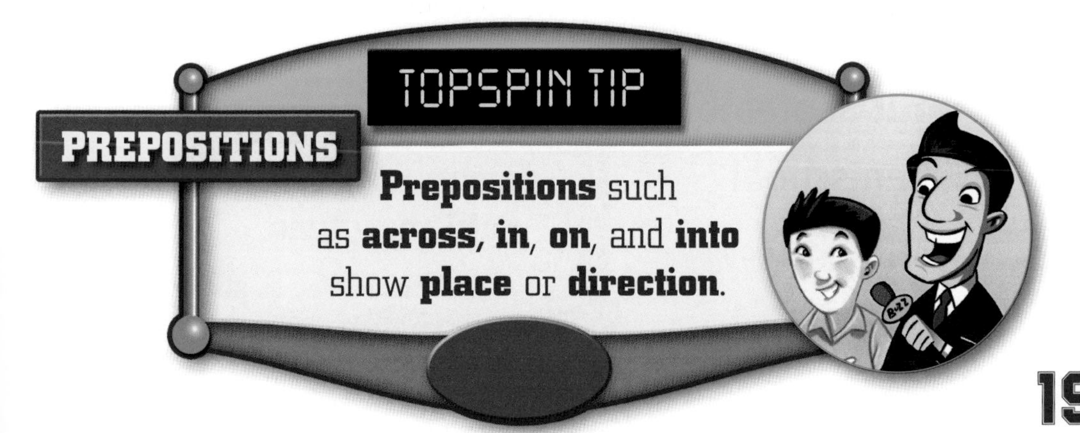

"Kevin ties his shoe **before** his serve," says Ken. "OK, now he's ready. POW! Lola smacks it back." Ken turns to Buzz. "**During** a fast volley, I always have trouble following the ball, Mr. Star."

"You're doing great, Ken," says Buzz. "I had the same problem when I started out. **After** the match, I'll give you some tips I've learned **since** that time. You'll be a pro **before** your next broadcast!"

"You mean I can help you on TV again?" Ken asks excitedly.

"Sure thing! You can be my assistant **until** September, when school starts," Buzz tells him.

TOPSPIN TIP

PREPOSITIONS

Prepositions such as **before**, **after**, **during**, **since**, and **until** show **time**.

BUZZ

"Here comes a drop shot **from** Kevin," says Ken. "Clay stretches to return it. Oh, no! The ball nicks the top **of** Clay's racquet!"

"It's game, set, and match **for** Kevin Wong and Bonnie Backspin!" Buzz says.

"Hooray!" shouts Ken.

"Let's go talk **with** Kevin **at** courtside," says Buzz. "He is signing autographs **near** that crowd of fans. Viewers, stay **with** P-L-A-Y TV **for** the presentation **of** the Junior Hot Shots trophy."

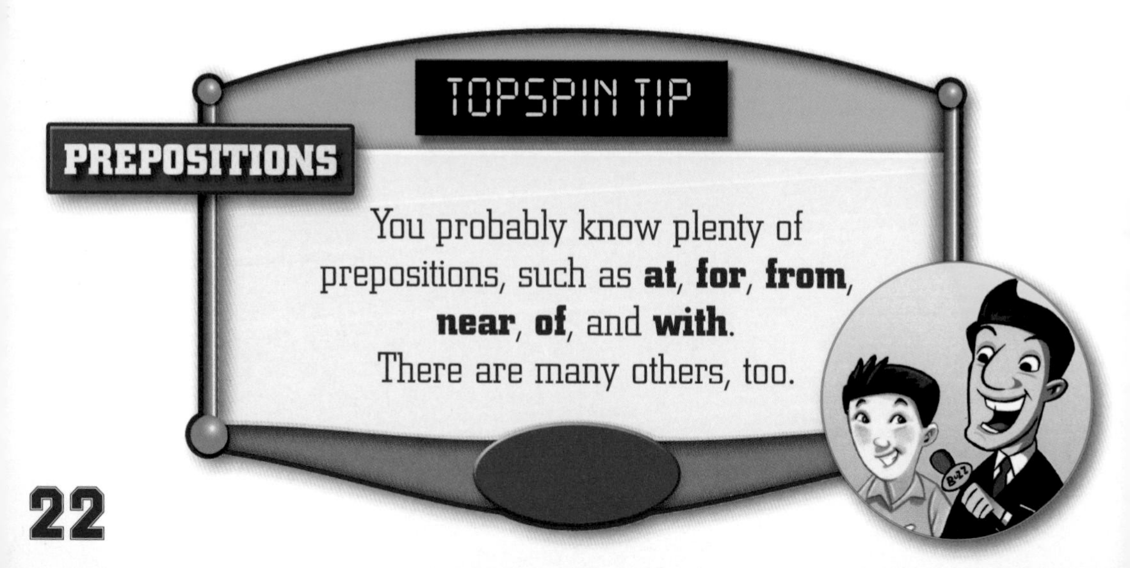

ALL-STAR ARTICLES

What Are Articles?

As Buzz and Ken walk through **the** crowd, people turn to look at **the** pair. "Great match!" **a** man calls out. "Can I take your picture?" asks **an** eager teenager.

Ken sighs heavily. "People think I'm Kevin, because we look alike. Even our friends sometimes have trouble telling us apart."

"That's **an** honest mistake," says Buzz.

Ken smiles slyly. "Sometimes we pretend to be each other, just for fun. Then people become really confused!"

"Well, I'm sure you have **a** few differences," says Buzz.

"Yes, my hair is straighter than Kevin's," Ken says, "and he has freckles on his cheeks."

"When people look closely, they'll see **the** differences," says Buzz. "Then they won't be confused anymore."

"At school, I get confused about **the** parts of speech. Conjunctions … prepositions … articles … Sometimes they all look alike, and I mix up **the** rules!" Ken shakes his head sadly.

"Just look closely, and you'll see some differences. You know that **a** conjunction joins words and that **a** preposition connects nouns or pronouns to other words in **a** sentence. What do articles do?" Buzz asks.

"They show that **a** noun is coming soon," Ken replies. "That's **an** easy question, Mr. Star!"

"And you're **a** good reporter, Ken. No, make that **an** ace reporter!" Buzz says with **a** smile.

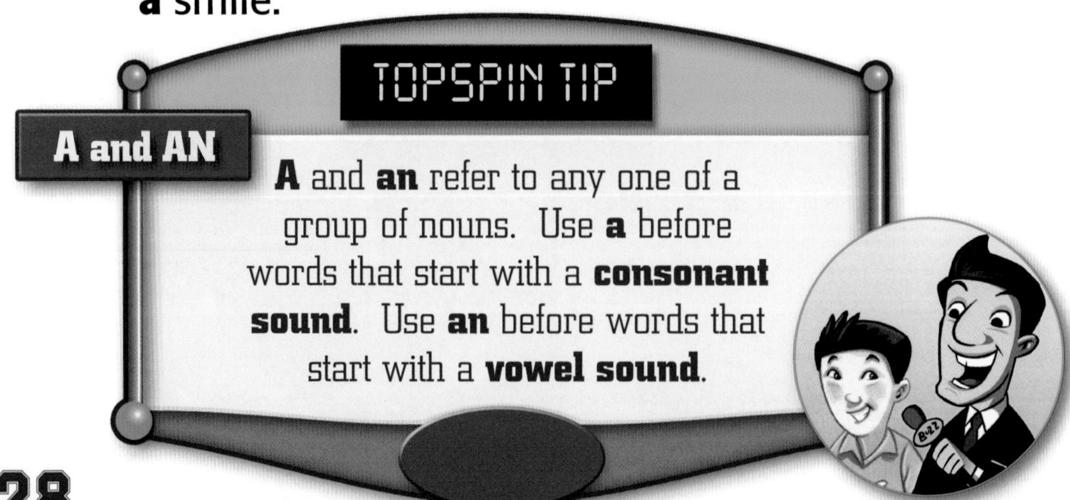

A and **an** refer to any one of a group of nouns. Use **a** before words that start with a **consonant sound**. Use **an** before words that start with a **vowel sound**.

"Thanks for **the** grammar tips, Mr. Star," says Ken." I had fun being **the** Junior Hot Shot kid reporter of **the** day."

"You were right on top of **the** action," Buzz answers. "You did a great job in **the** press box."

"Look!" says Ken, pointing to **the** court. "Kevin and Bonnie are accepting **the** Junior Hot Shots award. They are holding up **the** trophy and waving to **the** crowd. Wow, my brother's a star!"

"Kevin served up an ace on **the** court, but he's not **the** only all-star in **the** family," says Buzz. "You're pretty special yourself."

BUZZ STAR PLAYS BY THE RULES!

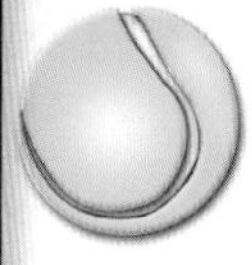

Conjunctions can join words.
Example: Mom **and** Dad don't play tennis.
Conjunctions can join groups of words.
Example: We'd better hurry **and** get up there.
Conjunctions can join groups of words that have a subject and a verb.
Example: Kevin is playing a mixed-doubles match, **and** his partner is Bonnie Backspin.

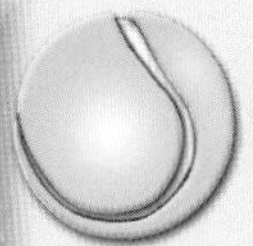

Prepositions link nouns or pronouns to other words in a sentence.
Example: Viewers, stay **with** us **for** the presentation **of** the trophy.

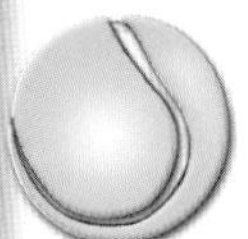

Prepositions can tell where something is or is going (place or direction).
Examples: Clay is **at** the baseline.
Lola ran **from** one side of the court **to** the other.

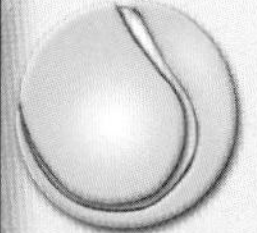

Prepositions can help tell when something is happening (time).
Example: Kevin signed autographs **after** the match.

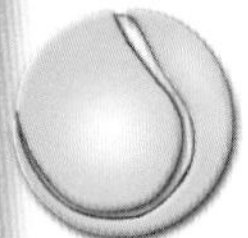

A, **an**, and **the** are **articles**. They signal that a noun is coming soon.
Examples: Would you like to get **a** snack before **the** match? I see **an** ice cream stand.

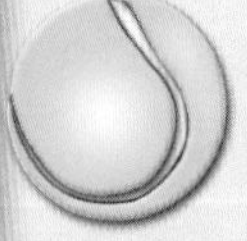

A and **an** refer to any one of a group of nouns. Use **a** before words that start with a consonant sound. Use **an** before words that start with a vowel sound.
Examples: Kevin is playing **a** mixed-doubles match.
He served up **an** ace.

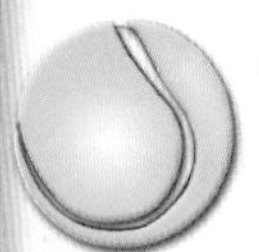

The refers to a specific, or particular, noun.
Example: Kevin and Bonnie won **the** Junior Hot Shots trophy.

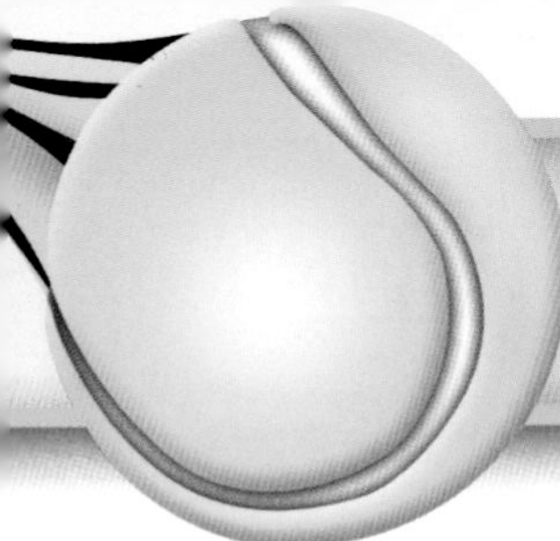

ALL-STAR ACTIVITY

Ken wrote a thank-you letter to Buzz Star.

Can you find all the conjunctions and prepositions in his letter?

Dear Mr. Star,

Thank you for taking me to the Junior Hot Shots tennis tournament at the Restless Racquet Tennis Club and letting me be a kid reporter. It was an exciting afternoon as the ball zoomed across the net during some long volleys. I don't know which part was more fun: watching my brother's match or being on TV. Announcing the action from the press box was cool!

Kevin and his partner, Bonnie, take lessons and practice together often. During their match, they made some amazing shots. Kevin's serves were always in bounds. Bonnie ran from one side of the court to the other. Clay and Lola were great competitors, but Kevin and Bonnie came out on top. They were tired after the match, but they had to pose for a picture and sign autographs.

Thank you for buying me an ice cream cone, too. I usually order a chocolate cone with sprinkles, but yesterday I decided to try an unusual flavor for a change. When you ordered a vanilla ice cream cone, I knew you were happy!

Your neighbor,
Ken Wong

On a piece of paper, list all of the **conjunctions** and **prepositions** in Ken's thank-you letter.

List all of the **articles** in Ken's note.

Turn the page to check your answers and to see how many points you scored!

ANSWER KEY

Did you find enough conjunctions and prepositions to win the match?

0–7: Foot Fault (oops!)

8–15: Game

16–23: Set

24–30: MATCH!

CONJUNCTIONS		PREPOSITIONS		
1. and	**7.** but	**13.** for	**19.** from	**25.** on
2. as	**8.** and	**14.** to	**20.** during	**26.** after
3. or	**9.** but	**15.** at	**21.** in	**27.** for
4. and	**10.** and	**16.** across	**22.** from	**28.** for
5. and	**11.** but	**17.** during	**23.** of	**29.** with
6. and	**12.** when	**18.** on	**24.** to	**30.** for

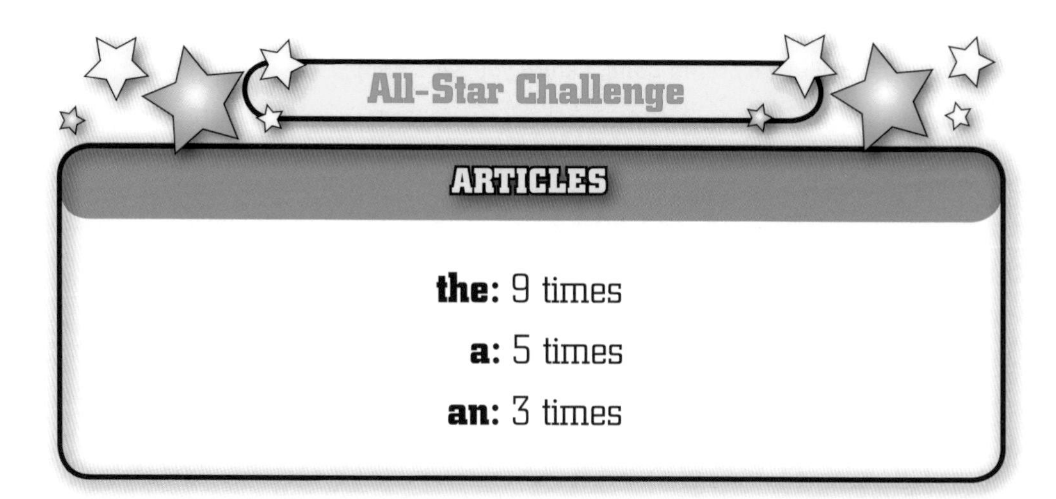

All-Star Challenge

ARTICLES

the: 9 times

a: 5 times

an: 3 times